The Entropy of Rocketman

poems by

Rita Anderson

Finishing Line Press
Georgetown, Kentucky

The Entropy of Rocketman

ACKNOWLEDGMENTS

"Vermeer's Pomegranate." Published in *The Stardust Gazette*, 2014-2015
Edition.
"Cultivating a Ruin." Published in *Inflight Magazine*. www.inflightlitmag.com/
issues/issue2, January 2015.
"Object Permanence." Published in *Words Work*. http://
wordsworkliteracyjournal.weebly.com/ Volume 5, Issue I. Summer 2012.
"Watched Pots." Published in *Explorations*, University of Alaska Press. 1994

Editor: Christen Kincaid

Cover Art: Steven Robert Anderson

Author Photo: Steven Robert Anderson

Cover Design: Elizabeth Maines

Printed in the USA on acid-free paper.
Order online: www.finishinglinepress.com
        also available on amazon.com

Author inquiries and mail orders:
Finishing Line Press
P. O. Box 1626
Georgetown, Kentucky 40324
U. S. A.

Table of Contents

Dedicated to the memory of John Hood,
beloved mentor and friend.

We preferred our dreams to our lives.

EARTH

Two Moons of August

On August 27, Mars will come within 34.65M miles of
Earth, looking like a second moon.

Joining porch shadow, I try not to wake
        the house I leave behind but moonlight
makes hiding unlikely, its glow too insistent
        to mention (but I feel giddy soaking in it).

Never before or again in this lifetime, the news warned,
        although I had warmed to the idea of another
planet's proximity, always open to illusion. Waiting and
        watching, I wrap my robe tighter despite heat that

nightfall didn't resolve, fresh from the dewiness of bed
        where you dozed, our dark dance as if in tribute
to how the bodies in space would revolve to find one another
        sometime after midnight (a false coupling to fool

the untooled eye). Peering, now, up at our young dreamer's
        window, I wondered if I should wake him for what
he wanted to witness, if not celebrate, with his own late-night
        appearance (*What about school in the morning?*
less complicated than was rousing him from sleep).

Although I was the sole witness, mine was not like his—
        a drive *to know*—the facts as wasted on me as was such
lunar radiance. I *did* marvel at the sky

but I always wound up counting clouds or trying to locate
        the only other intruder on the scene, something forlorn
but likewise earthbound chirping from the treetops.
        —The flight my thoughts took was *anything but* celestial,
traveling instead, too far back. . .

When reveling in peaceful surrounds I do not get lost in math
or astronomy but in human nature's web. *From the very beginning.*

It's the puzzle I return to, a riddle I can't answer:
Was there any way that first pair could have remained
in the magnificent garden, content with their lot? Or,
was one bound to nurture an ancient need for *more?*

Cultivating a Ruin

This is what I had wanted.
    [Isn't it?]
Bulldozers to rip out the grass
    in front of the house. Amazing
machines to transform the standard plot
    into a miniature Easter Island—
or an altar to a great sunken vessel
    dramatized in the yard next to the violets,
its bow and factory-rusted propellers
    jutting out of the dirt
like a hand in perpetual distress.

      : Let the neighbors stare.

The exotic is imported to disrupt tradition,
    as, unnaturally, we erect the *natural*,
a new but dilapidated thing
    only the *learned* could love.
An aquatic garden masterpiece
    straight out of the Romantics,
wild and overgrown (in prescribed fashion).
    This is the way I have loved you, outside the lines of reason,
searching for a blueprint I could pen you into.
    You, the bouquet of withered sunflowers
hung upside down, the crease in the pillowcase
    next to mine. *What hasn't been imbued*
with your memory like the bent page of a borrowed
    book you've forgotten you lent me?
I stew over the clue as if it were a secret
    your soul would not release, but then, with
an elaborate scrutiny, I flush it out
    until it is thrown, dead, into what
used to be the grass.

Imprinting

Conditioned to *want* this place, these vile city trees
with roots like exposed nerve desperate for cover, I
circle an old haunt as if I were a horse pinned to a carousel.

My pulse races at the corner store, but I drive slower
to savor the moment.—A decade later, the neighborhood
is worse but the wet sidewalk still reflects a neon Welcome.

I have no desire to alarm someone by idling this way at night
but I can't pull away. Not yet. Your house is dark
so I open the car window, hoping for a familiar smell

like a junkie hungry for anything that shoots me down
into the past but, although the same carved tire holds weeds
in the yard, the family I imagine inside has been gone for years.

The dog doesn't bark from the basement that reeked of her
confinement and, even if the worn carpet still climbs those stairs,
you don't dream in the room at the top. I can no longer lie

beside you in the dark, touching the hollow of your neck
where breath lifts and lowers the skin. Stirred by my presence,
you will not turn to return my caress. My desire won't

awaken a body that has moved on in time, where I am leashed.
—But, I am forced out of idle when the new owner flashes
the porch light and hollers that she has already called the police. . .

> *Lovers have moved over my body to leave impressions*, but
> their kisses are sand the memory of your touch washes away.

Vermeer's Pomegranate
(Ars Poetica)

The most beautiful nights should be lived
not painted (or painted *through* living, as if

electric moments were a book of moving portraits).
Last night, the moon could have made me forget

my name, amazing how long I'd refused
its impact and, yet, time always slows

> when we're in-between memories.

The combination of the abstract *theme* of dishes,
the everyday *realism* of sandwich-making, and the way

the moon's gray light caught me pathetically clutching
my chest, looking skywards, is grotesque but I abandoned

work anyways and went out to join the breeze,
a last call of birds.

> —Again, *that* which is extraordinary
> should be captured in your pale lemon arms,
>
> not in oils with a brush (or by words on a page),
> but I have not painted in as long as I have not embraced
>
> you, because art starts in desire and desire has left
> the building. But. Last night! . . .

Since selection is part of art's process, I took a walk
to find you—and did: Last night the green moon *was* you

(I am making a discreet point here). I moved into the blue
fog of past until you held my hand as we talked of summer.

I stopped to make out the heavy fruit which bent a vine
over the fence, when you plucked the largest and gave it to me,

shoulders brushing as we kissed,
nighttime like a lost love letter. . .But,

I should not have breathed it in, this dark street
littered with pages from an old calendar.

>—It is wrong to suggest that these props,
>although allegorical, are mere symbols
>
>that support my own meaning. That I chose to return
>to a time long out of date—for the maps taped to the trees
>
>and windshields of parked cars showed not the region
>that existed but the provinces as they were before
>
>truce was declared and the treaty signed—reveals
>that, as a work of art, Love Is A Failure.

But, *last night,* the moon (*Verbotten!*) was a fragrance
that makes fools of lovers whose oaths open the dykes

to flood the land, leading nearby countries to war.
And who can sleep when the wound of love is

an overripe orange swollen in the sky,
barely hanging on?

WATER

Anatomy of a Lighthouse

:There is *something to be said* about change
for change's sake, clean sheets on the line
crisp as wafers in the thrashing wind. Somehow,
the outdoors is trapped in as I press my cheek
against the fabric and breathe in the surf.

. . . And about *contradictions* because although I enjoy
swimming I seldom do. In so many faulty ways
we credit ourselves *due*, claiming health because once,
every day for a month, we rode a bike, sighing
nostalgically now whenever cyclists pass.
We think we *belong*. Deaf to their laughter
and how their fit bodies navigate inclines up
a flowering seaside cliff, we still imagine
an effortless glide among them. In the end,
there is no reality to it but much comfort.

During landlocked Midwestern winters
where steel firms but corn farms survive,
the ocean is a hope I could hurt myself with,
a cruel illusion that spoils the good I may hold
in my hand.—Besides, what do I know
of the ocean other than that it houses whales and Red Tide?
What peace do I think would rise from a landscape
where water gnaws at the edges? (*So why, then,*
seek refuge in you, from dreams that perfect
memory but can't console?)

I've read that waves run in patterns
and only in the ocean, where lighthouses line the shallows,
a reach out through fog. But why these wave-swept beacons
over and over so many years after the wreckage? And why,
when you never liked the water, does the image recur
of you as a lighthouse? *Mine.* Something solid
and protective, a foreign role for us both.

But I won't play the widow,
a pouting statue affixed to the rooftop. (Does being lost and
finding a way out make us survivors—even if we still don't see
the world as it is but as we are?)
I envisioned love a place I could map, but that
continent drowned
with you. Our love was a boat I floated on that thinned to a raft
before falling apart
when faith in your faithfulness—like the dark air around me—
grew too heavy to carry,
a light too faint to follow.

Object Permanence

Just as I am sure you must be *around*,
sharing a piece of the invisible universe,
        somewhere, a gorilla sweats in the shade,
eating aphids from a leafless stick. . .
        Not counting trips to the bathroom,
I am down to four hours of sleep
        and when I dream I'm with Houdini,
swimming in an ocean of liquid ice.
        We keep our eyes open, waving
our hands like windshield blades
        to recover the exit in the fist-thick ice
overhead. He is better at floating
        close to the top where you can
almost catch a breath between waves,
        but it will be over soon: For all of his magic,
There is no escaping an ironic end.
        In the middle of the ordeal,
I remember that *This isn't my tragedy*
        and I'm rescued to a warm room
where I remove my brain to soak it
        like you could a pair of dentures.—In
the morning when I slip into the kitchen
        to pour my son a second bowl of cereal,
he no longer cries, afraid that because
        I have exceeded his sight I've disappeared,
and when my right hand hides the red ball
        behind the abyss of my back, he anticipates
the left hand's finding it, perhaps too certain now
        of its return.

Divorce

From the dark water swarming with fins
a boatload of the slowest fish is scooped
into the transport, eyes gaping, mouths

stretched for oxygen. Gills work the air
like frantic vents opening and closing,
bodies thrashing in self-defense (*counterattack/*

discomfort/denial); however, this is not a drill
but the fire. And here's the catch: if they stay
in the crowded tank every one dies, but

the alternative is painful and a swifter
end more likely. When moving
fish from hatcheries into the aquariums,

rivers, and streams where they will spend
uncertain futures, a saline solution is added
to the water, throwing the fish into a fight

for their lives—a state of strangulation
and paralysis short of *fins-up*. Face the facts:
fish prefer darkness, climbing each other and

clustering to avoid death. Hiding is a way of life
so there will never be a good time. Change is neither
welcomed nor bloodless, *even when it is rescue*.

Still, it must be easier for bass. Airborne and in transit,
they may miss regular meals but not one searches
for meaning, only water clean enough to survive.

Watched Pots

On Sundays when my son is with his father,
I keep busy. There are toilets to scrub, papers

to grade. Ironing. A litany of things in need
of attention, I forward my distraction to them.

But this flurry isn't smokescreen enough
to swallow the loneliness that envelops me.

Finally, I collapse into a chair on the patio
with a drink. The stump of the oak they cut

down last year is shrouded by a sheet
of flowing green that shot up immediately

afterwards like a scab.—I want Nature's
resilience, to know how to salvage a loss

and spin it off into an altar of healing, but how
can I parlay my mistakes into things of beauty

when I can't even say I've learned a lesson
half the time? The sun has set before my mind

settles, the night breeze blowing through
my blouse. Still, I wait and pray to be tired

enough to sleep. More than another chance,
I want wisdom to know what to do with it.

In Medias Res

A woman appears, stranded
        on the shore of your fire circle.
Although the face is already a map,
        she longs to tell her story—and you
have *time* on your hands. Rubbing
        them over the blaze, you encourage
her to pull up a log (Where to start?). *So there I was. . .*
        will not set this stage, but you tire of her
preparation, the false starts. Shaking
        like a dog losing the river he has exited,
you look her in the eye—which seems to work, loose
        lines of her epic coming in like waves
from out to sea, lifting your weariness down
        every waterway, against each crag, until
you wish the story that took so long to start
        would end, but it doesn't. Infinity seems
destined to play itself out in an endless curve
        and crest of her wave. Your feet long
to touch bottom, something solid to walk away
        on, but the tide swallows you into the plot.
Reluctant Witness made Character in this
        untidy storyline, you protest, the words
drumming into your chest like water torture
        until they form a puddle that you can see
yourself within. Suddenly (It was *not* so sudden),
        you recognize that your pain is equal to hers,
maybe greater. Her confession little more than yours
        squeezed into a discarded bottle, a story you
did not have the heart to tell. *Save the whales!*
        you holler, vowing to draft a resolution,
to man the oars and help row home.

FIRE

The Flood, the Burning

(Post-Katrina, New Orleans)

On top of the mountain of moldy carpet he has yanked
from his home, my neighbor makes up his own verses
of "Michael Row Your Boat Ashore," plucking a banjo—
a dry find in a load of junk. *What else can you do* when
the neighborhood is wrecked and we're still trying to live there?

I open my car window to escape the lemon smell that masks
an underscent of wet dog, remnants of the last hurricane.
As I hunt a place to park between the piles of garbage, I'm reminded
of the game we played as kids: If you could only take
ten things from a burning house, what would you save?

Yesterday, you called to tell me that your car was lost,
water to the dashboard also claiming books
you were too tired to unload since moving out days before.
Your voice flutters when you say you found my
picture in a favorite book you had rescued: *It's a sign,*
my face tucked into a poem called, "Save the Boat". . .

I stop to count the bodies, up and down the street, filing in
and out of their houses like work ants trying to salvage
the hive. When a cat springs out from behind the shed, I scream.
(But I am also that animal—a wild creature now, seeking
refuge in uninvited spaces, and stealing hope from your journal,
words

you never spoke.) What I didn't tell you when you called, *couldn't,*
is that I'm done scavenging for love. Listening to your
confession, I was ashamed at how little I missed of what was gone.
Our old house—my home—*is* empty but intact,
the love I had for you, a charred frame where a portrait
once hung.

On Wanting to See Asher Lev's Trees

I. Asher Lev

Freedom starts with an exercise in perspective
and shadow. In a borrowed studio, you learn

not to look away, studying first the body then
its branches. From trees it is not much of a stretch

to crosses. Your thoughts follow your brush
into the hollows, learning by error how

a blueish hue makes a flower fragile, and
a face, gaunt, until *you* are the obsession

that explodes the ceiling in your teacher's
loft, your roots tearing out the sewer pipes.

Until hunger isn't easy like it used to be.
This one is never sated. Like an increasing stream

of gas that feeds a flame, the appetite flares.
It is torture, peeling back the layers,

madness in hunting the truth into a corner
until—veering away from a collision—you

wheel into the disaster you were meant to find:
You saved your parents by martyring them.

II. Chaim Potok

"Asher's paintings converted onlookers."
They *do not exist* but how I have imagined

his sorrowful trees, as you describe. How I'd
like to stumble into a gallery and—reaching past

the red velvet that ropes me out—feel the flesh of his
oils on canvas. Like the bleeding woman in the Bible,

I am sure I would be healed. *But.* "Asher" isn't real.
He's only a symbol of the writer's betrayal. Yours

is the pain that radiates from his eyes.
The pain you say he paints.—I am not

that interested in you: the monster, created,
appeals to me more than its maker.

I have met many artists I had admired
until I met them. How disappointing

they stood in contrast to their work—
the *imagined*, a force of its own, like

plants that had outgrown clay pots.

Collision

It's news every winter:
>an elderly couple from Iowa takes
>a wrong turn at night, coursing up
>a down slope and into oncoming traffic that
>provides instant admission to the Afterlife.

But what if accidents were rare,
>the astounding statistic that so *few* occurred
>and that fatalities weren't as common as toast,
>millions of roads jammed with weary drivers
>who push to end trips in record time, making unannounced
>merges, forced de-acceleration on a dime?

Still, the simple science of, "A body in motion wants
>to stay in motion" doesn't fix a face that
>has crashed so quickly through a windshield
>that the smile—lost to the pain of recovery like
>an unhinged bumper—is never traded for a scream.
>Surgeons can extract the shards and scars will replace the
past,
>but the event remains a wound, miniscule bits
>worming to the surface like hidden sin that festers.

Perhaps the real tragedy is that
>after stains fade, nothing is left but a sad paradox:
>You can rescue the girl from the ravaged car,
>but you cannot save her from the wreck. Or
>make her stop loving the driver.

Rebus

She stands naked as a celery stalk in grandmother's kitchen,
       holding a blue apple. (A teacher, she knows
the apple is blue because it is not getting enough oxygen.)

Quickly, he dresses in clothes like puzzle pieces that do not fit
       together because his wife—across town—texts,
punching in their wedding date as message. A deep freeze is

coming so he zips his coat, giving the girl in the family
       kitchen a parting peck on the apple. (It is still blue.)
Careful not to drop the apple, which rocks in her palm

with the effort, she moves behind him to lock the door,
       which is liquid fire. Alone again, alone, she tries
to sleep without disturbing the blue apple but it sweats

in her hand—which almost rests atop a king-sized
       comforter that doesn't. (*Can you imagine?*)
Home now, he disrobes again and dreams

behind the wife, his snakelike body
       spooning her aluminum frame.
No part of him is blue.

Marriage

Mystery lies in the miniscule.

If a noble gas wants for and needs nothing,
        its outer shell filled, complete, then
by design Uranium 238 is volatile, seductive.

        Although it possesses special properties
which illuminate, it favors the destructive, its very
        nature leaning towards disintegration through

detonation. Rare, pure elements, fully encumbered
        cannot bear added weight which exhausts
the strong nuclear force. Unable to hold it together

        a Chain Reaction results, one heavy atom
setting off the next as radio (re)active neutrons—
        bombarded with more—split apart,

        shooting out even more neutrons. Overly
        charged, decaying.

        But,

line the chamber with Uranium 235 and
it absorbs the extra neutrons the other emits.

The *lesser* element—identical in all ways except
this—not only disables the monster
explosion but is itself enriched: it becomes more

excited. In symbiotic complement, what
was crowded thins. Problems resolve:
the agitated is channeled, activating the inert,

a miraculous combination.

SKY

Parallax, 1972

I stared at the sun without blinking. Believing
    my brother's claim that it emitted vitamins
that would strengthen my sight, I strained until
    my eyes burned, tearing then closing, but even
under the moist lids the roiling fireball blazed on
    as if singed into the retina. On my back
in the back of the paneled station wagon,
    I was the nebula between my older brothers'
more solid bodies: they didn't need me
    and they couldn't shake me, our feet
floating over our heads
    as we simulated space flight.
We would hang upside down from tree limbs
    to practice weightlessness and crashland
into the pool with our coats on.
    I followed them in the same way
that the moon trailed our car on trips,
    as if it were a balloon tied to the tailpipe.
When the second brother protested,
    Girls aren't allowed on the moon,
the older one conceded,
    We'll just make her carry all the stuff.

Caravaggio Paints the Football Stadium, a Skyscraper, a Storm

In the mind of this dreamer, the only window
is closed [and seems always to have been so].

I. Stadium
In the backfield, a human tank waits for the snap,
but from here he's all tortured grimace, a dark smudge
for eyes. The turn of last century was at hand,

his family—engulfed by a complex ensemble—already
a thing of the past. Sounds bounce from miniature
speakers over bleachers of hot dogs and chocolate,

but (*to keep an emphasis on the essential*) the beautiful
boy is the show. And here, before love has found him,
he can allow himself to slake his thirst

and he desires to surpass himself. The spectators,
alive only in their hopes for him, hold their painted
breaths and hang on the edge, frozen in the stands

like a backdrop of rotten fruit
and fake leaves juxtaposed with fresh. . .

II. Skyscraper & Storm
From a top floor of glass walls, the geometry
of downtown and heaven itself are the backdrop,
au current, to three figures cast in silhouette.

They huddle as a storm erupts from black clouds.
(They too were a city in the throes of transformation.)
"We should get to solid ground," he shouts. "Or

at least get out of the window," she mumbles as
father, mother, and son empty the tower—but each
pursues a separate path to safety. (Was the family

tired of a common life and life in common? Or is
theirs the kind of mystical crisis a painter cannot
capture?) Running free, now, in the street, they don't

see the Lightning Bolt that comes for them. It splits the sky
to end the chiaroscuro forever, the rogue blaze that follows
them showing us—the onlookers—that, There's no escaping destiny.

Foremost in the portrait stands a provocative Angel
who strokes the Lamb that will replace the child.

The Entropy of Rocketman

Pluck a feather from a crow
at the window, growing blacker in the rain.
(Or, lean in and pull a page from my book:
This is not your *best hour* or your last.)
Ride it out.

Uninvited, sorrow lands
on every fence, in time, but jettisoned as
you are in the churning centrifuge you cannot see
beyond the madness of the hub. All
you know has been taken from you

and continues to fall off like spent metal
from the vessel's burnt-out core because
you cannot control your speed or which parts will unravel, when.
Then, what seems vital splits—if only this
were not your only transport.

All you hold is this moment but you don't

want it, the one thing you'd like to shed.
Rocketman, you could not stay in space if you wanted to.
But. When the spinning stops and dreams return, picture the
pepper seeds rooted, the Rose of Sharon awaiting your
return, the one careful hands have helped to join
the earth, branching into cloud.

And, for the heavens-that-surround-you's sake,
discard the map you misread and others' judgment,
recall instead what wouldn't be here without your vision,
which exceeds their grasp: There is more to you than fire and
sky.

Remember, too, the divine pull of love's
gravity and that you are part starfish.

That Last Week (In the Airport Café, Hours Early)

I blow ripples into my coffee to erase my reflection
while you talk about *regrets*, and the Ten Things
        you would do before you died: an icy jeep ride
to help deliver plasma to Argentinian MASH units—
        or at least gas fare—and the three-hundred dollars
you should've lent a client for Christmas. . . Your wife
        and grown children no longer listening, you bend my ear
(a woman you never liked) and I study my hands, finding
        the sadness inescapable, but how right it was that
we should have been *there* then, a million lives buzzing
        around us like rush hour on a human expressway,
the zippered faces of those like me leaving, lives bulging
        out of bags, contrasted against the smiles of the
incoming, a palpable care shared with loved-ones. It takes
        years but, now, I understand your longing, which whirs
within me, as do visions of Pamplonian Bulls you will never run,
        and I am filled with the rush of *unchanced* things, the
waste.

When Beggars Die There Are No Comets Seen*

It's odd, sometimes, the things that attract us—
        a lover whose last name is French-Moon,
the yachtlike acreage of a stranger's shoe, a footnote
        that stays with you longer than the plot:

A friend who drank too much green wine in Spain is haunted
        by a woman who stripped (relieving herself of more
than the bondage of clothing) in front of a landmark fountain
        that was captured in brochures as a four-star must-see.

Instead, I watched her for hours. . .

Although I know my friend's fear, I do not tip my hand
        by touching hers because we, too, have strayed
from the path like travelers who had been to distant stars
        but settled for what we could hold onto.

If our infrequent lunches are forgettable, then what
        do I do with her Undulating Woman in the Fountain
who was not a foreign curio but a warm soul (who now
        belongs to me too), lapping at the fallen universe?

        And, What If the undrawn line is the truest parameter,
        one we cannot erase but would never cross?

*from *Julius Caesar*

On slow days like this

it ought to pour. On the café patio
where I've come to end an affair
with isolation, I think I'm hungry until
I have the muffin on a plate, jelly glistening
on a post where an old man stares puzzled
by the honor box. "Number 36!" and a woman
returns to the counter, wishing aloud for rain
as she passes an underage couple who is smoking.
*This is your world in which we grow and we will
grow to hate you,* his shirt reads when I bum
a cigarette. But there is, finally, a breeze
on which my thoughts drift to the time
I spent helping new mothers. . . A hired hand,
I held their babies, sautéed tofu, and listened
to difficult stories of more difficult labors. Just
two or three days at this crux in their lives
and I was gone, but I wonder if they think of me,
as I do them: the woman who stenciled photos
of pets onto stationery, the mother I held
while she cried, refusing to touch her infant, and
how her husband wept as he wrote my check.
The thing is, I have always wanted *in*—
and *out*—but I haven't succeeded. On slow days
like this, the melancholy filters in like garden
scents let in through an open window. Lives
that have smudged against mine like blossoms
that bleed fragrance when it rains.

Rita Anderson, an award-winning playwright and poet, was poetry editor of *Ellipsis* (literary publication, University of New Orleans). Rita won the Houston Poetry Festival, the Gerreighty Prize, the Robert F. Gibbons Poetry Award, the Cheyney Award, and an award from the Academy of American Poets. Her poems have been published in *Spoon River Poetry Review*, *EVENT Magazine (British Columbia)*, *The Blueshift Journal*, *Blotterature*, *Words Work*, *Transcendence*, *PHIction*, *Persona (50th Anniversary Edition)*, *The Artful Mind*, *Di-Verse-City: An Austin Poetry Anthology*, *Inflight Magazine (Paper Plane Pilots Publishing)*, *DLC Literary Journal*, *Cahoodaloodaling*, *The Stardust Gazette*, and *Explorations* (University of Alaska Press). Contact Rita at www.rita-anderson.com